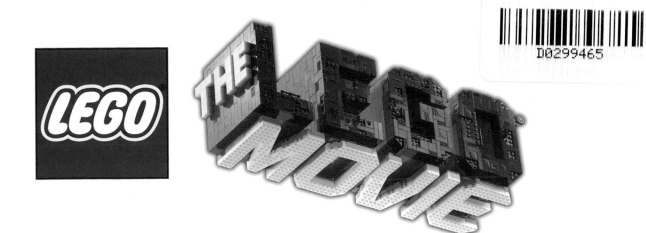

LEGO THE LEGO MOVIE

ULTIMATE STICKER COLLECTION

How to use this book

Read the captions, then find the sticker that best fits the space. (HInt: check the sticker label for clues!)

•

Don't forget that your stickers can be stuck down and peeled off again.

•

There are lots of fantastic extra stickers for creating your own scenes throughout the book!

DK

LONDON, NEW YORK, MELBOURNE, MUNICH, and DELHI

Written and edited by David Fentiman
Designed by Lauren Rosier

First published in Great Britain in 2014 by
Dorling Kindersley Limited
80 Strand, London WC2R 0RL

10 9 8 7 6 5 4 3 2 1
001-193687-Jan/14

Page design copyright © 2014 Dorling Kindersley Limited
LEGO, the LEGO logo, the Brick and the Knob configurations,
and the Minifigure are trademarks of the LEGO Group.
© 2014 The LEGO Group
Produced by Dorling Kindersley Limited under licence from the LEGO Group.

A CIP catalogue record for this book
is available from the British Library.

ISBN: 978-1-40934-515-2

Colour reproduction by Altaimage, UK
Printed and bound by L-Rex Printing Co., Ltd, China.

Discover more at
www.dk.com
www.LEGO.com

Emmet

Emmet really wants to be a good Bricksburg citizen, and have everyone like him, so he always follows instructions that tell him how. He's cheerful and enthusiastic, and may seem like a normal guy, but heroes can come from the least likely places...

Emmet

Emmet likes the same things as everyone else: TV, local sports teams and pop music. He is just a regular, normal, ordinary guy.

Hard Hat Emmet

Emmet is a construction worker on a building site in Bricksburg. It's the perfect job for someone who loves instructions.

Instructions

Lord Business's Octan Corporation makes instructions for everything. They display the warning: "Failure to follow instructions may result in a sad and unfulfilling life".

Piece of Resistance

The Piece of Resistance is a legendary artefact and the only thing that can save the Universe. And now it's stuck on Emmet's back!

Where are my Pants?

Emmet's favourite TV show is *Where are my Pants?* The episodes might be predictable, but everyone in Bricksburg loves it.

Step 4

Emmet only ever reads one book – it's called *How To: Fit In, Have Everybody Like You, And Always Be Happy*. Step 4 is to take a shower every morning.

Good morning city!

The Special?

According to prophecy, the one who finds the Piece of Resistance is the Special – the greatest, most important person in the universe.

EMMET

Bricksburg

Bricksburg is like any other city – its citizens get up in the morning and go to work. They keep the city running smoothly by following Lord Business's rules, and think they have perfect lives. They don't realise what Lord Business is planning...

Master Builder Wyldstyle

Wyldstyle refuses to follow Lord Business's instructions. She is super-creative, and wants to do good in the world.

Plumber Joe

Joe loves his job. In fact, if he can't fix a leak or blockage in less than half an hour, he'll do it for free!

A Model Citizen

Emmet always obeys the rules, and never goes looking for trouble. Unfortunately for Emmet, trouble will find him!

Plumbing Van

Joe's plumbing van is full of wacky tools, so he's ready to solve any plumbing problem.

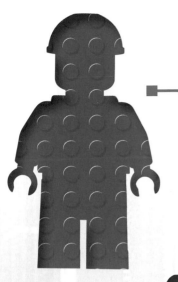

Frank the Foreman

Bricksburg is being totally rebuilt by Lord Business. Frank the Foreman is in charge of the construction site.

Gail the Construction Worker

Gail is the perkiest member of Frank's construction crew, and is very skilled with her pneumatic drill.

Alfie the Apprentice

Joe is teaching Alfie everything there is to know about plumbing. One day Alfie hopes to have his own van.

Dr McScrubs

Being a doctor isn't easy, but Dr McScrubs manages to care for his patients and look handsome at the same time.

Executive Ellen

Ellen is your typical businesswoman. Smart, well dressed and always on time for meetings.

Blaze Firefighter

Blaze is a hero. When there's trouble he's always on the scene, saving people, pets and property.

Kebab Bob

Bob's kebabs might not look particularly appetising, but they are the tastiest in town. It's best not to ask what the ingredients are...

5

City Life

Everything in Bricksburg is made by Lord Business, and the citizens love following his instructions. For now, they don't want anything to change, but if someone inspires them, who knows what could happen!

Ice Cream Van

The giant ice cream cone on the van's roof makes going round sharp corners quite difficult.

Bad Cop and the Super Secret Police

Lord Business's authority is enforced by the Super Secret Police, led by his most loyal employee – Bad Cop.

Ice Cream Mike

Everyone in Bricksburg loves Mike's ice cream, even though it tastes a little bit artificial.

Mrs Scratchen-Post

Even Mrs Scratchen-Post doesn't know for sure how many cats she has, but it's definitely a lot...

Ice Cream Jo

Jo helps out with selling ice creams, and she can't help singing along to the awesome ice cream van music.

Cardio Carrie

The instructions tell citizens of Bricksburg to stay healthy, so Carrie goes jogging every morning, whatever the weather.

Garbage Truck

A clean city is a well-behaved city, so Octan garbage trucks are a common sight.

Gordon Zola

Chef Gordon Zola could be more creative with his food, but he just follows the recipes every time.

Garbage Man Grant

Grant loves his job. He's been doing it for so long, he's now immune to all but the most disgusting smells.

I'm not sure I know how to make that...

Garbage Man Dan

Garbage Man Dan prefers driving the truck to handling garbage, which he usually leaves to Grant.

Lord Business

As President of the Octan Corporation, and the World, Lord Business is used to getting what he wants. And what he wants right now is to control the Universe. If he can't be stopped, things are going to get very sticky around here.

President Business

Lord Business also has a business to run. As President Business, he controls all of the popular music, TV and everything else in Bricksburg.

Evil Schemes

President Business wants everything to be ordered and sensible. He hates anything weird, and wants to keep things the way they are, permanently.

Executron

Lord Business doesn't trust people to work for him, so he uses a team of robot "Executrons" to run his business.

Lord Business

A helmet, a cape and a giant pair of big boys' pants transform President Business into the terrifying Lord Business!

Micro Manager

Lord Business created a fleet of micro managers to rebuild the world exactly the way he wants it. They're programmed to take apart anything creative.

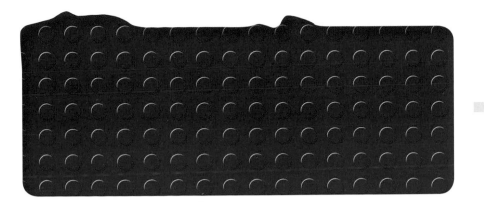

Taco Tuesday!

Taco Tuesday is supposedly when every citizen of Bricksburg will get a free taco. It's actually when Lord Business plans to end the world as they know it!

Master Builder Vitruvius

The mystical Vitruvius once guarded the Kragle, but lost his sight when Lord Business attacked him and stole it.

Behold! The power of the KRAGLE!

The Kragle

Lord Business plans to use this mysterious (and very sticky) weapon to freeze all of existence.

Bad Cop

There are two sides to this cop: one good, and one bad – but Bad Cop's bad side is definitely the one in control. He's Lord Business's most loyal henchman, and he'll do whatever it takes to catch Emmet and retrieve the Piece of Resistance.

Policed to Meet You!

Bad Cop is a tough interrogator, and commands Lord Business's Super Secret Police Force.

Freeze!

Bad Cop is quick to go for his laser when chasing suspects – he prefers to shoot first and ask questions later.

Good Cop

Underneath all the meanness of Bad Cop, there is another cop – a good cop. For now, though, Bad Cop is in charge.

Jet-Car

Bad Cop's car isn't any ordinary police vehicle. At the push of a button, it changes into a flying jet-car!

Ma Cop

Bad Cop's parents, Ma and Pa Cop, are the first to be exposed to the Kragle weapon, when Lord Business forces Bad Cop to freeze them.

Pa Cop

Pa Cop is a small town cop without much in the way of ambition. He hopes his son is doing well in the big city.

> **RED ALERT!**
> I need everyone to go after the **SPECIAL!**

Scribble Face Bad Cop

When Lord Business betrays him, Bad Cop realises the error of his ways, and draws a new good cop face on himself.

Robo Croc

Bad Cop even has robotic police crocodiles to help chase after Emmet and Wyldstyle.

Wyldstyle

Emmet thinks Wyldstyle is beautiful, creative, brave and cool. She is a Master Builder – a hero with an amazing imagination, able to build anything out of anything. It's up to her to rescue Emmet, and help him defeat evil Lord Business.

Melting Room

Emmet has been sent to the Melting Room by Bad Cop. He's in trouble if no one can save him!

Urban Chic

As a fugitive from the law, Wyldstyle favours dark, hooded clothing, with a few suitably artistic tweaks.

Skilled Warrior

As well as being an amazing Master Builder, Wyldstyle is a super-agile and fearless fighter.

Super Cycle

To escape from Bad Cop, Wyldstyle uses her Master Building powers to build this awesome flaming motorcycle!

S.W.A.T. Car

This 4x4 police S.W.A.T. car is super-fast and heavily armed with missiles and explosives.

Bad Cop

His name pretty much sums this guy up, and he'll stop at nothing to capture Emmet and Wyldstyle.

Scared Emmet

Emmet is just a regular, normal, ordinary guy. He doesn't know what's going on. Why do people want to melt him?

Robo S.W.A.T.

Lord Business's robo S.W.A.T.s can't be bargained with, can't be reasoned with, and don't feel fear, so watch out!

The Old West

The Old West is home to rough cowboys, rowdy saloons and robots. Lots of robots. Emmet and Wyldstyle try to find the wizard called Vitruvius, but end up being chased by the mean Sheriff Not-a-robot and his dangerous Deputron.

Hands up!

The Deputron is the Sheriff's henchman. He's a straight shooter with his laser, and is obsessed with dynamite.

Getaway Glider

This crazy hang glider helps Emmet and Wyldstyle to escape from Lord Business's robotic minions!

Cactus

It just wouldn't be the Old West without a cactus. Watch out though – it's spiky...

Sheriff's Hat

Any self-respecting sheriff needs two things. A badge... and a big hat with a star on it.

Trusty Steed

The Sheriff uses his horse to chase down fugitives and outlaws. It's fast, but doesn't corner very well.

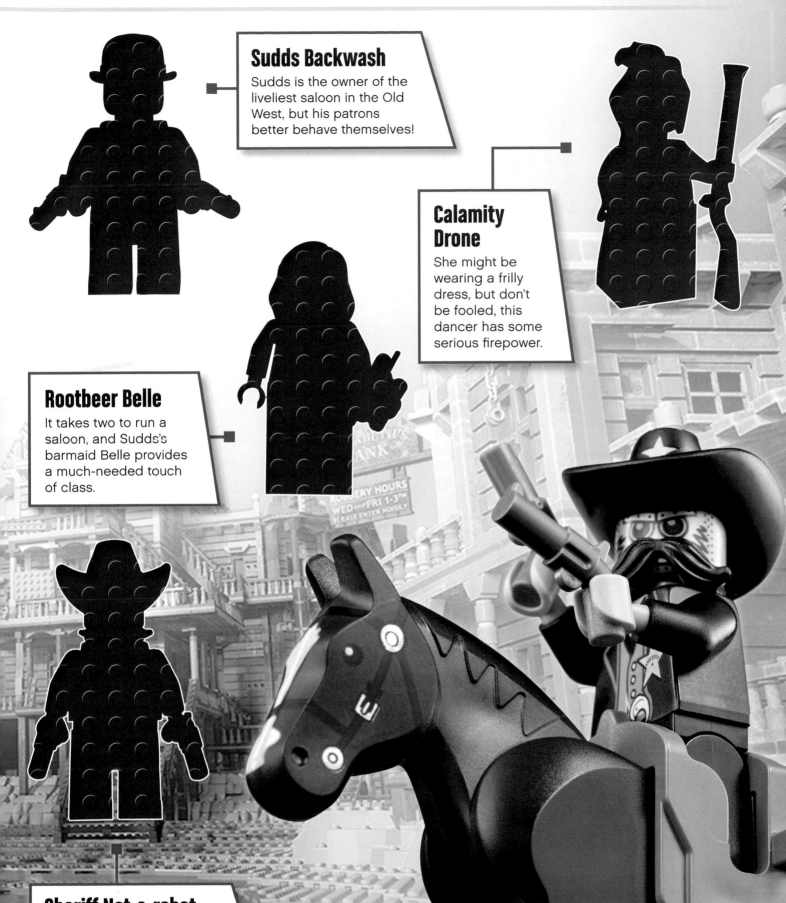

Sudds Backwash

Sudds is the owner of the liveliest saloon in the Old West, but his patrons better behave themselves!

Calamity Drone

She might be wearing a frilly dress, but don't be fooled, this dancer has some serious firepower.

Rootbeer Belle

It takes two to run a saloon, and Sudds's barmaid Belle provides a much-needed touch of class.

Sheriff Not-a-robot

The Sheriff always gets his man, but with a moustache that big, he must be hiding something underneath it...

Middle Zealand

Middle Zealand is a magical land of knights, castles and dragons. What it lacks in indoor plumbing it makes up for in adventure! It's also the gateway to the secret realm of Cloud Cuckooland, meeting place of the Master Builders.

Sir Stackabrick

As lord of the castle, Sir Stackabrick is a shining example of chivalry and knightly honour.

Gallant Guard

It's a tough life being a guard: long hours, low pay and regular dragon attacks.

Castle Stronghold

With its sturdy gate, tall towers and wall-mounted crossbows, this stronghold is a difficult nut to crack.

Catapult

This mighty catapult can make the walls of even the strongest tower crumble into rubble!

Use your extra stickers to create your own LEGO® Movie adventure!

Cloud Cuckooland

Hidden in the clouds, Cloud Cuckooland is the happiest, most positive and most creative place in the whole Universe. It is also the home of Princess Unikitty, who thinks that any idea is a good idea, except the not happy ones.

Unikitty

Half unicorn, half kitty, all cute – Unikitty makes sure that there is no negativity in Cloud Cuckooland.

Friends?

At first, Wyldstyle finds Emmet's lack of creativity frustrating, but she slowly realises there is more to him than meets the eye.

Cloud Cuckoo Palace

With its colourful twirling pinwheels and flowers, Unikitty's Palace is cute and adorable, just like her.

Angry Kitty

Being positive all the time takes its toll on Unikitty. When her hidden rage is unleashed, look out!

Tracking Device

Emmet doesn't realise that Bad Cop has attached a tracking device to him, and has followed him to Cloud Cuckooland.

Metal Beard

Metal Beard the pirate lost his body in an attack on Lord Business's lair. He struggles to stay positive about things.

Flower Catapult

Even the weapons in Cloud Cuckooland look cute. This catapult fires sparkly flowers.

Master Builder Benny

Benny is a classic 1980s spaceman. He's a happy guy, but all he really wants to do is build spaceships.

Cute Snail

Snails don't always have to be horrible and slimy – anything with eyes this big can't help but be lovable.

Here in Cloud Cuckooland there are no rules!

19

Inside Octan Tower

Octan Tower is Lord Business's headquarters, where he plots his evil schemes. Reaching all the way up into outer space, it's probably the scariest office building in the Universe. Getting inside is not easy – or very sensible.

Shocking Behaviour!

As part of his evil project, Lord Business captures Emmet and attaches him to a giant battery!

Biznis Kitty

In order to break into Octan Tower, Unikitty uses this smart corporate disguise.

Mr Big Boy Pants

Lord Business thinks that just because he's really tall, he gets to be the boss. Perhaps someone should tell him that the bigger you are, the harder you fall.

The Think Tank

Lord Business puts the captured Master Builders into his Think Tank, where he uses their creativity to develop even more evil plans.

Robo Skeleton

As well as micro managers and Executrons, Octan Tower is full of scary Robo Skeletons!

Velma Staplebot

Velma is Lord Business's overbearing office assistant. If people don't have an appointment, she has been known to destroy them.

Vitruvius

Vitruvius joins the mission to break into Octan Tower. He might look old, but he prefers to be called "experienced".

TV Studio

Octan Tower is where they film Emmet's favourite TV show: *Where are my Pants?*

Metal Beard

Avast mateys! Metal Beard might just be a head these days, but he was once the scourge of the seven seas. His broken body has been replaced with ship parts of every kind, and he is obsessed with getting revenge on Lord Business.

Yaaar!
Metal Beard's body is made up of cannons, anchors and even sharks. He couldn't be more shipshape if he tried.

Save Me Metal Beard!
A micro manager has got Frank the Foreman! If Metal Beard can't save him, no one can!

Heavy Metal Duel
Metal Beard is big enough to take on one of Lord Business's micro managers in a one-on-one duel!

Use your extra stickers to create your own LEGO® Movie adventure!

Creative Armada

It's time to put a stop to Lord Business's fiendish plan! All across the land, Wyldstyle's message of creativity has helped people to transform things into incredible combat craft. Now they can fight back against Lord Business!

Saloon Bi-plane

Winging its way in from the Old West, Sudds Backwash's saloon bi-plane will blow up the bad guys with dynamite!

Flying Kebab Stand

Kebab Bob has decided to make a stand against evil. A flying kebab stand to be precise.

Kebab Rocket

This greasy projectile is so hot, it's guaranteed to melt right through anything it hits!

Castle Cavalry

The Knight's stronghold has been transformed into a marvellous medieval flying machine!

Howdy pardners! Anyone fancy a rootbeer?

SALOON

Plunger Missile

Once a plunger has hit its target, it's nearly impossible to remove, which has the added bonus of making the target look very silly.

Flying Flusher

Plumber Joe and Alfie the Apprentice have converted their van into a dousing dive bomber with plunger missiles.

Sudds to the Rescue!

Executive Ellen is being chased by a micro manager! Sudds must dive in and save her!

Crazy Contraptions

Yet more mad machines join the fight against Lord Business! With just a little creativity, even everyday things can become crazy contraptions! These vehicles all have surprises in store for wicked Lord Business and his micro managers.

Fire Truck Mech

Blaze Firefighter has turned his fire truck into a fearsome fighting machine! The high-powered water cannons make short work of robotic foes.

Ice Cream Machine

What could be cooler than a flying ice cream machine firing ice cream missiles? Freeze, sucker!

Ice Lolly Missile

Ice to see you! These flying frozen missiles make short work of the micro managers, and taste nice too!

Carrot Bomb

Carrots can help people to see in the dark, and they also make excellent anti-robot weapons. What a useful vegetable.

Windmill Helicopter

Old West farmer Hank Haystack has brought his windmill to the big city. Its vegetable bombs will make a mess of anything underneath!

Sometimes you have to fight fire with fire!

Trash Chomper

The garbage men are ready to take out the trash! This chomper's jaws can make a meal out of a micro manager.

The Master Builders

The Master Builders are the bravest heroes in the whole Universe. They may not look special, but each one is a source of incredible creative energy, with the power to use their surroundings to build anything they can imagine.

Wyldstyle

Wyldstyle is one of the most powerful Master Builders. Her creations are super-cool and have a unique urban style.

Policeman

If there's trouble, dial 999 and the Policeman will come to the rescue. He's ready to lay down the law.

Circus Clown

Some people are scared of clowns, but they've nothing to fear from this one. He just wants to build the world's biggest big top.

Magician

Whatever he's hiding underneath his hat, you can bet he also has some magical building tricks up his sleeves.

Artist

This talented artist can make a beautiful masterpiece, simply by waving his paintbrush.

Punk Rocker

How does he keep his hair sticking up like that, and why does everything he makes have skulls on?

Yeti

If you need something built out of ice, you should get in touch with the Yeti – his ice brick igloos are really impressive.

Hazmat Guy

Don't tell him, but there's actually a hole in his suit. He would be very upset if he found out!

Benny

Benny only ever wants to build one thing: Spaceships! Spaceships! Spaceships!

Panda Guy

It must be hot inside that Panda suit! It's not clear whether Panda Guy is a mascot for a sports team, or if he just likes wearing it.

Amazing Heroes

Some Master Builders aren't just incredible builders, they have awesome powers too, like super strength or super speed, or super invisibility, or super... positivity. Every one of these guys is amazing. That's the important thing.

Master Builder Unikitty

Whenever Unikitty builds anything, she can't help but make it totally adorable. Awww!

Green Ninja

The Green Ninja can disappear in a puff of smoke, and use his golden katana swords to defeat evil.

Superman

Superman – the Man of Steel – is the greatest hero of all. He's always ready to save the world.

Swamp Creature

His home might be in the dark, dingy swamps, but this monster is full of bright ideas for building!

Marsha

Building things underwater must be quite hard, but as queen of the Mermaids, Marsha has mastered it.

Wonder Woman

Wonder Woman uses her Lasso of Truth to catch bad guys. She also has an invisible jet, but she often has trouble finding it.

Ghost

What goes bump in the night? Probably this ghost, as he likes using his poltergeist powers to build spooky things.

Green Lantern

Green Lantern's powers come from a special ring, which he can use to build anything he wants out of thin air!

Johnny Thunder

This brave explorer is on a mission of adventure! Nowhere is too dangerous or too remote for Johnny.

Batman

The caped crusader has come to battle Lord Business. But he only works in black (and sometimes very, very dark grey).

Historical Figures

Some Master Builders come all the way from the distant past. They certainly have interesting tales to tell about the good old days, but their finest hour is when they help defeat Lord Business and save the Universe!

Shakespeare

To build, or not to build, what a silly question! This playwright has a brand new play – *Much Ado about Building.*

Abraham Lincoln

As well as being president, Abraham Lincoln has lots of useful building tips: "a house divided against itself cannot stand!"

Forestman

Whether he's saving the world or robbing the rich to pay the poor, the Forestman always wears stylish green tights.

Lady Liberty

This French lady's favourite things include the freedom to build, and the pursuit of happiness through creativity.

Egyptian Queen

The queen only builds things in the shape of a pyramid, which is quite difficult if you only have square bricks.

Stickers

Flying Flusher

©2014 LEGO

©2014 LEGO

Garbage Truck

Octan RUBBISH   G 349

RP 70805

©2014 LEGO

Plumbing Van

©2014 LEGO

©2014 LEGO

©2014 LEGO

Octan's JOE'S PLUMBING

Master Builder Benny

©2014 LEGO

Friends?

©2014 LEGO

A Model Citizen

©2014 LEGO

©2014 LEGO

©2014 LEGO

FIRE 70813

Fire Truck Mech

EMMET

Mrs Scratchen-Post

©2014 LEGO

©2014 LEGO

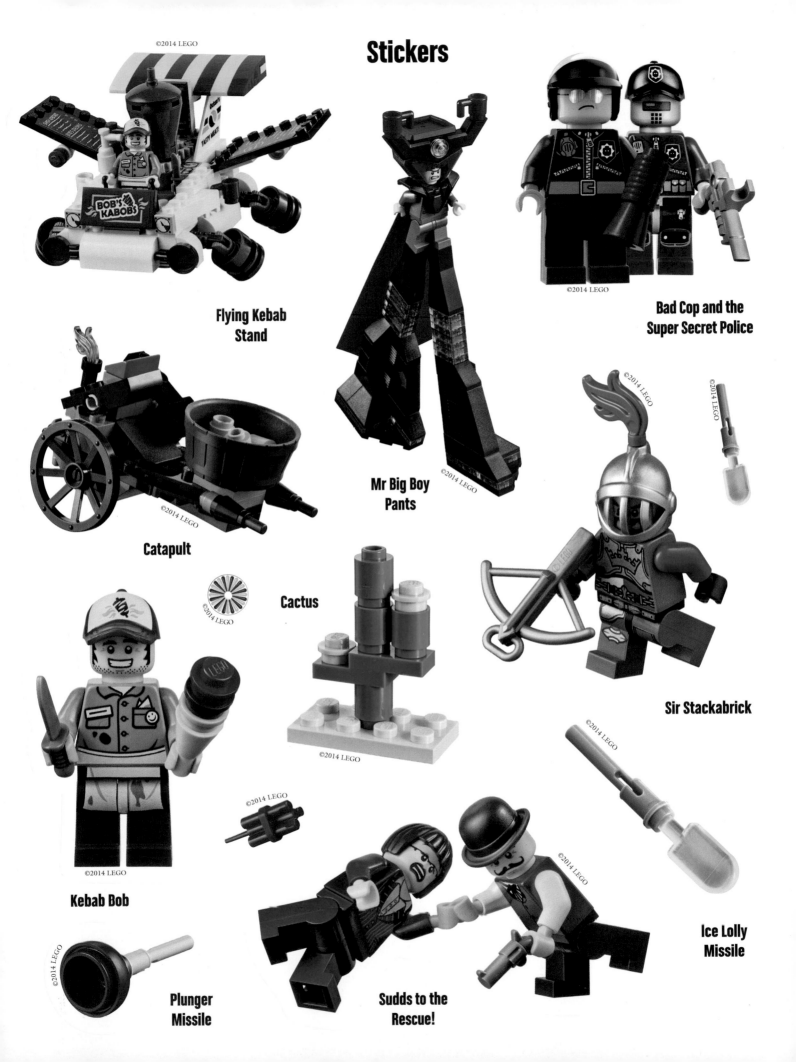

Stickers

Flying Kebab Stand

Mr Big Boy Pants

Bad Cop and the Super Secret Police

Catapult

Cactus

Sir Stackabrick

Kebab Bob

Plunger Missile

Sudds to the Rescue!

Ice Lolly Missile

©2014 LEGO

Stickers

Trusty Steed

©2014 LEGO

©2014 LEGO

Robo Skeleton

©2014 LEGO

©2014 LEGO

Plumber Joe

©2014 LEGO

©2014 LEGO

©2014 LEGO

©2014 LEGO

©2014 LEGO

Master Builder Wyldstyle

©2014 LEGO

Sheriff Not-a-robot

©2014 LEGO

Ice Cream Jo

©2014 LEGO

©2014 LEGO

©2014 LEGO

Flower Catapult

©2014 LEGO

Cute Snail

©2014 LEGO

©2014 LEGO

Trash Chomper

Castle
Cavalry

Stickers

Kebab
Rocket

Gallant Guard

Shocking Behaviour!

Cardio
Carrie

Ice Cream
Machine

Dr
McScrubs

Tracking
Device

Frank the
Foreman

Garbage
Man Dan

Stickers

Saloon
Bi-plane

Ice Cream
Van

Carrot
Bomb

Getaway
Glider

Vitruvius

Executive Ellen

Windmill
Helicopter

Calamity Drone

Biznis Kitty

Stickers

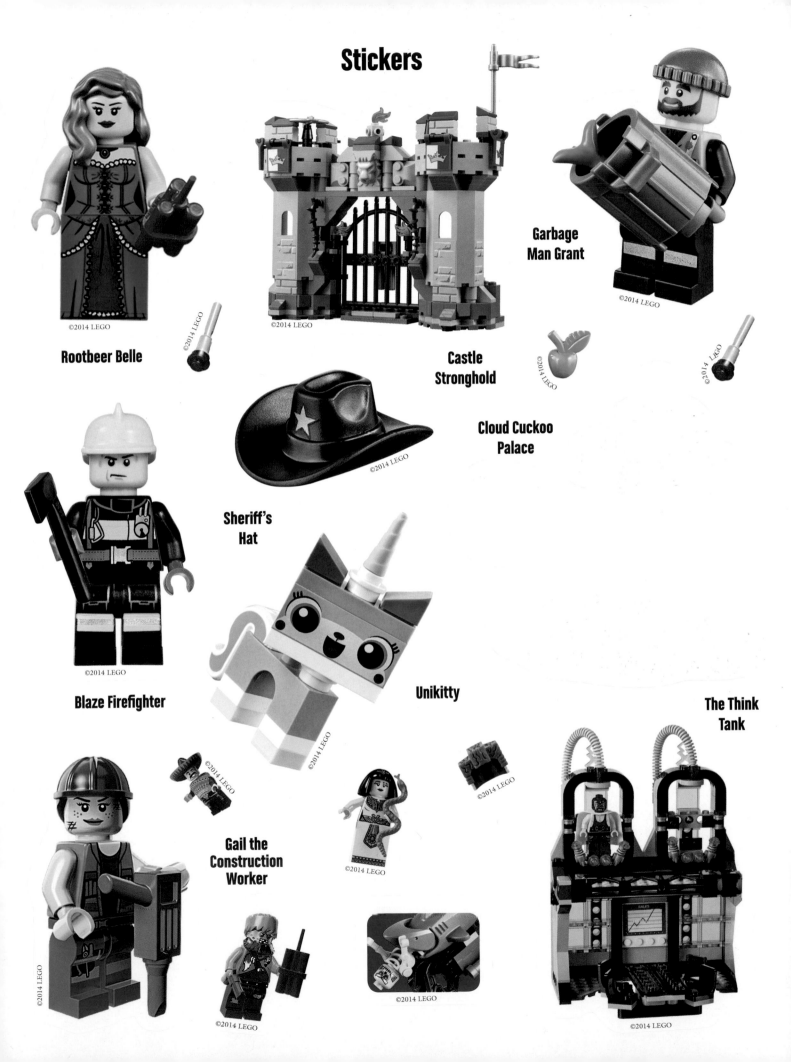

Rootbeer Belle

Castle Stronghold

Garbage Man Grant

Cloud Cuckoo Palace

Sheriff's Hat

Blaze Firefighter

Unikitty

The Think Tank

Gail the Construction Worker

Stickers

Metal Beard

©2014 LEGO

©2014 LEGO

©2014 LEGO

©2014 LEGO

©2014 LEGO

TV Studio

Super Secret Plan: "TACO TUESDAY"

Velma Staplebot

Alfie the Apprentice

Hands Up!

©2014 LEGO

©2014 LEGO

©2014 LEGO

©2014 LEGO

Ice Cream Mike

MIKE

©2014 LEGO

©2014 LEGO

©2014 LEGO

Angry Kitty

©2014 LEGO

©2014 LEGO

Gordon Zola

©2014 LEGO

©2014 LEGO

©2014 LEGO

Sudds Backwash

Stickers

Policed to
Meet You!

Panda Guy

Johnny
Thunder

Swamp Creature

S.W.A.T.
Car

Yeti

Hazmat Guy

Egyptian
Queen

Artist

Micro
Manager

Emmet

©2014 LEGO

Stickers

Scared Emmet

©2014 LEGO

Magician

©2014 LEGO

©2014 LEGO

©2014 LEGO

©2014 LEGO

©2014 LEGO

Punk Rocker

©2014 LEGO

Green Lantern

©2014 LEGO

©2014 LEGO

Instructions

©2014 LEGO

©2014 LEGO

©2014 LEGO

©2014 LEGO

Abraham Lincoln

©2014 LEGO

Four score and seven years ago...

Heavy Metal Duel

Stickers

President Business

Robo S.W.A.T.

Benny

Piece of Resistance

Wyldstyle

Urban Chic

Good Cop

Green Ninja

Lady Liberty

Pa Cop

Stickers

Wonder Woman

The Kragle

Forestman

Bad Cop

Yaaar!

Evil Schemes

Step 4

Melting Room

©2014 LEGO

Stickers

Executron

Skilled Warrior

Master Builder Vitruvius

Scribble Face Bad Cop

Freeze!

Batman

Ghost

Circus Clown

Stickers

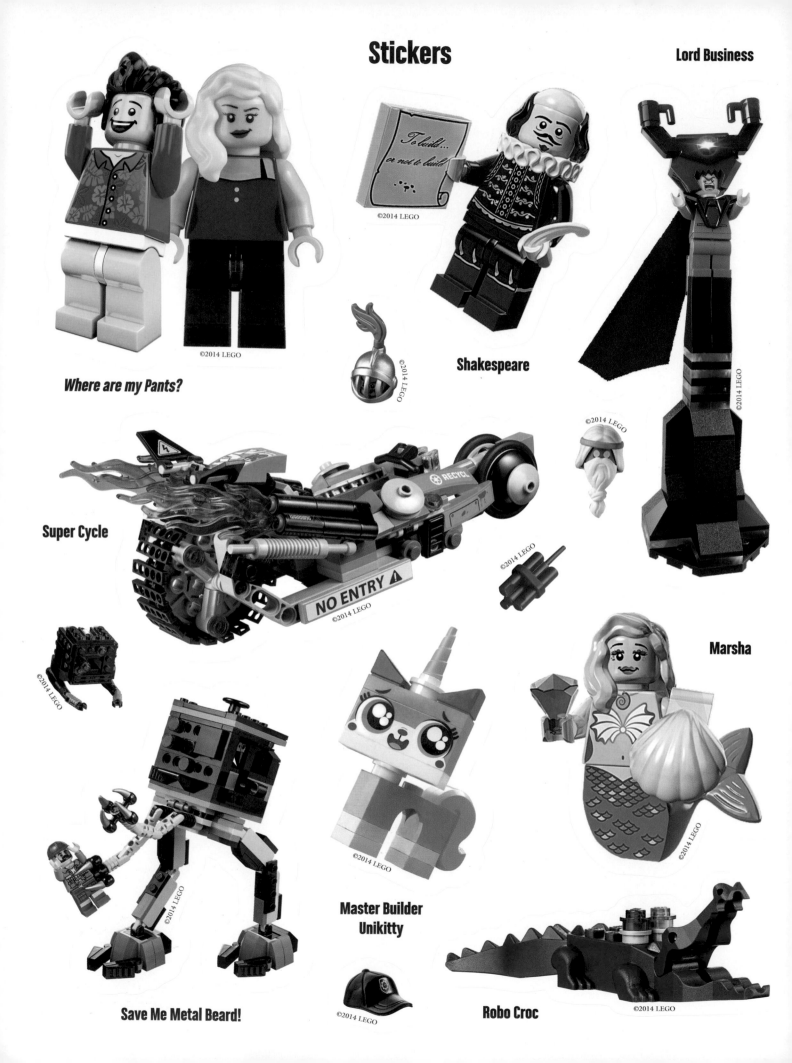

Lord Business

©2014 LEGO

Where are my Pants?

©2014 LEGO

Shakespeare

©2014 LEGO

©2014 LEGO

Super Cycle

NO ENTRY

©2014 LEGO

©2014 LEGO

©2014 LEGO

Marsha

©2014 LEGO

©2014 LEGO

Master Builder
Unikitty

©2014 LEGO

Save Me Metal Beard!

©2014 LEGO

Robo Croc

©2014 LEGO

©2014 LEGO

Stickers

©2014 LEGO

Superman

Ma Cop

Hard Hat Emmet

Policeman

Taco Tuesday!

The Special?

Jet-Car

Extra Stickers

©2014 LEGO

©2014 LEGO

©2014 LEGO

Octan RUBBISH   G 349

RP 70805

©2014 LEGO

©2014 LEGO

©2014 LEGO

©2014 LEGO

Octan's JOE'S PLUMBING

JOE'S PLUMBING

LB 11 256

©2014 LEGO

©2014 LEGO

©2014 LEGO

©2014 LEGO

FIRE 70813

©2014 LEGO

©2014 LEGO

Extra Stickers

Extra Stickers

©2014 LEGO

Extra Stickers

©2014 LEGO

Extra Stickers

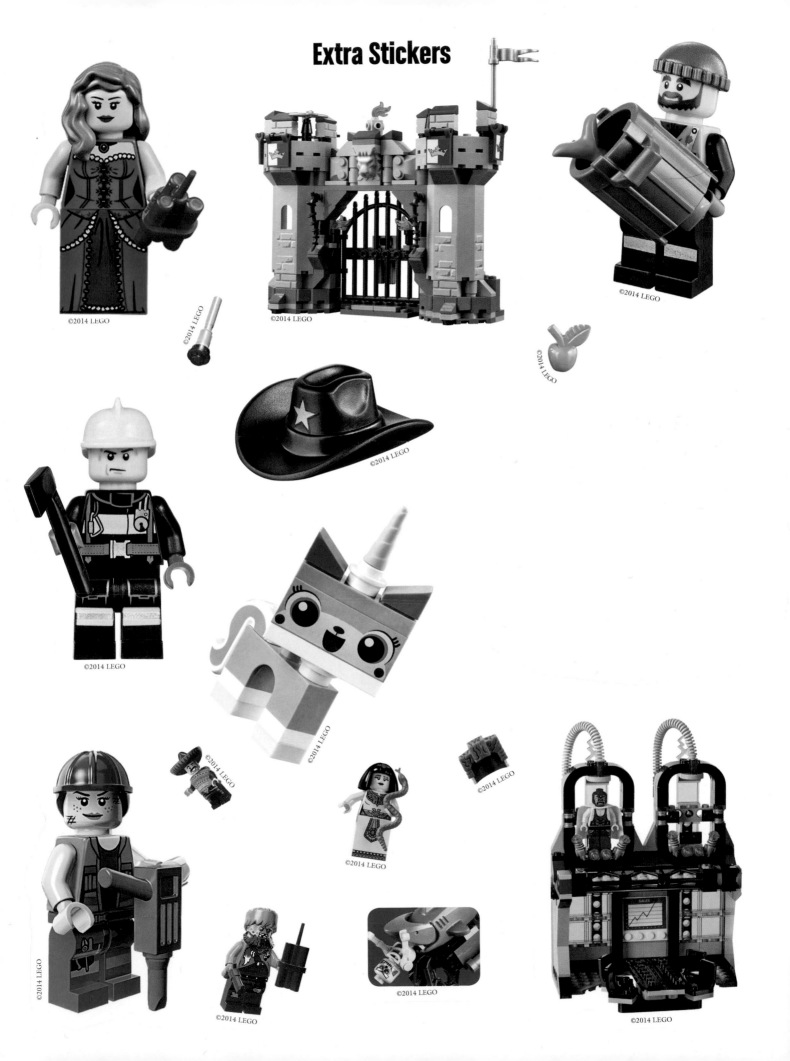

Extra Stickers

©2014 LEGO

Extra Stickers

Extra Stickers

©2014 LEGO

Extra Stickers

©2014 LEGO

Extra Stickers

©2014 LEGO

Extra Stickers

©2014 LEGO

Extra Stickers

©2014 LEGO

Extra Stickers

©2014 LEGO

Extra Stickers

©2014 LEGO

©2014 LEGO

©2014 LEGO

©2014 LEGO

©2014 LEGO

©2014 LEGO

©2014 LEGO

©2014 LEGO

©2014 LEGO

©2014 LEGO

©2014 LEGO

Extra Stickers

Extra Stickers